Fiddle Time Joggers

a first book of very easy pieces for violin

Kathy and David Blackwell

Illustrations by Martin Remphry

Welcome to the Third Edition of **Fiddle Time Joggers**. You'll find:

- open string pieces and tunes using the finger pattern 0–1–23–4
- duets—start with the staves marked ☆; come back and play the other part later!
- three new pieces, replacing nos. 3, 29, and 44
- audio play-along and backing (accompaniment only) tracks available to download from www.oup.com/ftjoggers3e or to access on principal streaming platforms
- audio practice tracks (recorded at a slower tempo) for some pieces, also for downloading/streaming
- piano and violin accompaniments available separately in printed collections
- An ideal book to use alongside *Fiddle Time Starters*
- a book for violin that's also compatible with *Viola Time Joggers*

OXFORD
UNIVERSITY PRESS

Great Clarendon Street, Oxford OX2 6DP, England
This collection © Oxford University Press 1998, 2001, 2005, 2013, and 2022
Unless marked otherwise, all pieces (music and words) are by Kathy and David Blackwell and are
© Oxford University Press. All traditional pieces are arranged by Kathy and David Blackwell and are
© Oxford University Press. Unauthorized arrangement or photocopying of this copyright material is ILLEGAL.

Kathy and David Blackwell have asserted their right under the Copyright,
Designs and Patents Act, 1988, to be identified as the Composers of this Work.

Impression: 1

ISBN: 978-0-19-355940-0

Music and text origination by Julia Bovee.
Printed in Great Britain

Contents

Open strings

1 Bow down, O Belinda

American folk tune

pizz.

arco

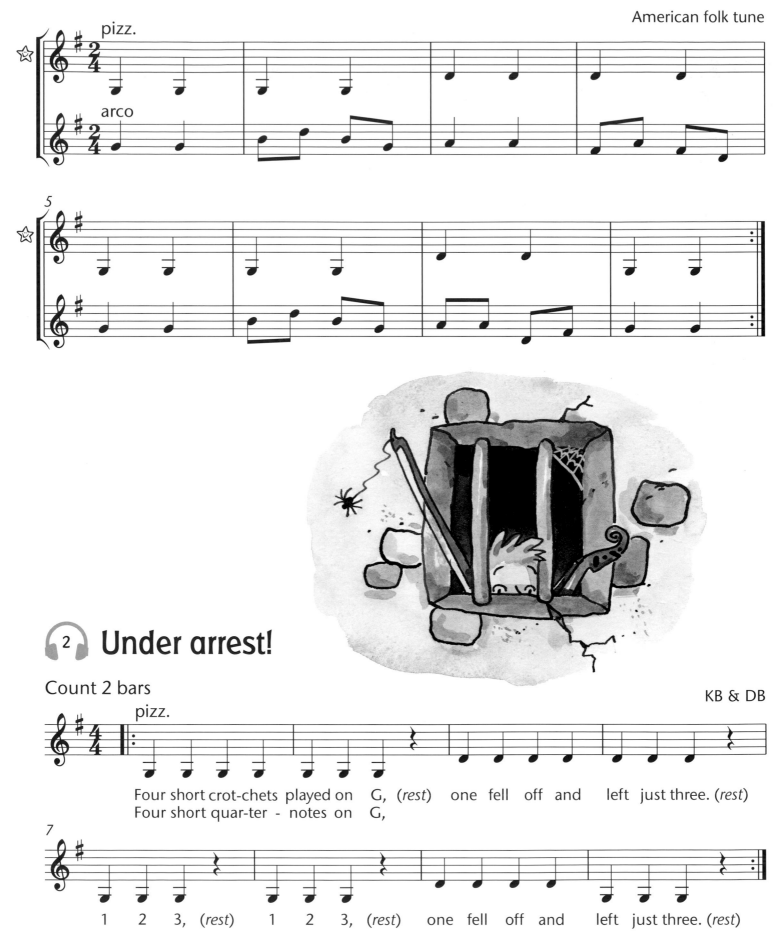

2 Under arrest!

Count 2 bars

KB & DB

pizz.

Four short crot-chets played on G, (rest) one fell off and left just three. (rest)
Four short quar-ter - notes on G,

1 2 3, (rest) 1 2 3, (rest) one fell off and left just three. (rest)

Say the word 'rest' quietly to yourself as you play.

🎧 3 Someone plucks, someone bows

Traditional
Words KB & DB

Down, up goes the bow, when we're play-ing fast or slow;

down, up goes the bow, when we're play-ing high or low.

🎧 4 Down up

KB & DB

Count 2 bars

Down up E string, down up A string, down up D string, down up G string;

* _____ Play the A and end with D.

* Fill in the letter names of these notes.

5

5 Two in a boat

American folk tune

6 London Bridge

English folk tune

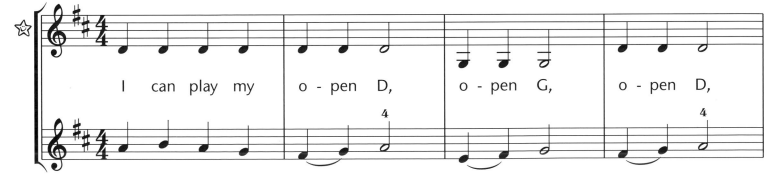

I can play my o - pen D, o - pen G, o - pen D,

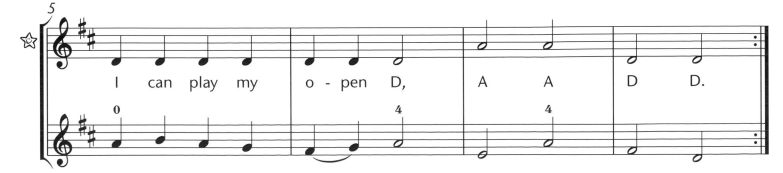

I can play my o - pen D, A A D D.

🎧 7 Fast lane

Count 2 bars

KB & DB

Fast

Try even faster the second time through!

🎧 48 Practice tempo

🎧 8 In flight

Count 4 bars

KB & DB

Calmly

In the rests, let your bow make a circle as you swoop and soar like a bird.

🎧 9 Lift off!

KB & DB

Lift your bow off in each of the rests and let it orbit! (Make a circle with your right arm.)

Try playing this rhythm variation
in each bar:

Or - bit round the moon.   (*etc.*)

🎧 10 Katie's waltz

Count 4 bars

KB & DB

KB & DB

Can you play what I play? D D E E

Fine

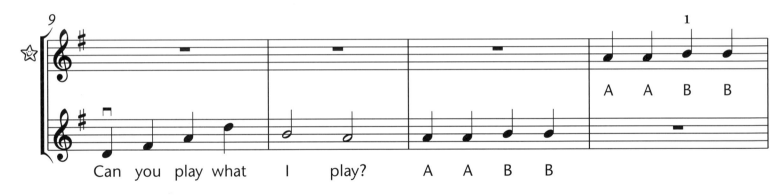

Can you play what I play? Play it now with me.

Can you play what I play? A A B B

D.C. al Fine

Can you play what I play? Play it now with me.

10

12 Tap dancer

Count 2 bars

KB & DB

Steadily

7

Fine

11

D.𝄋 al Fine

* Hold the bow upright and tap the screw end of the bow on your music stand.

13 Rhythm fever

Count 2 bars

KB & DB

Rock tempo

Rhy-thm fe-ver, 1 2 3 4 feel the beat, 1 2 3 4

7

feel the rhy-thm, 1 2 3 4 in your feet. 1 2 3 4 Feel the rhy-thm

12

as you play it, feel the beat go 1 2 3 4 Rhy-thm fe-ver,

16

1 2 3 4 rhy-thm fe-ver, 1 2 3 4 rhy-thm fe-ver, oh yeah!

49 Practice tempo

14 Here it comes!

KB & DB

Through the teeth and past the gums, so watch out, tum-my, here it comes!

Through the teeth and past the gums, so watch out, tum-my, here it comes!

* Think of a foody rhythm and play it on these notes.

Here is an idea to start you off:

Fish and chips and ice cream.

15 So there!

Count 4 bars

KB & DB

Brightly

So there!

16 🎧 Rowing boat

Gently

KB & DB

Getting slower

17 🎧 Ally bally

Scottish folk tune

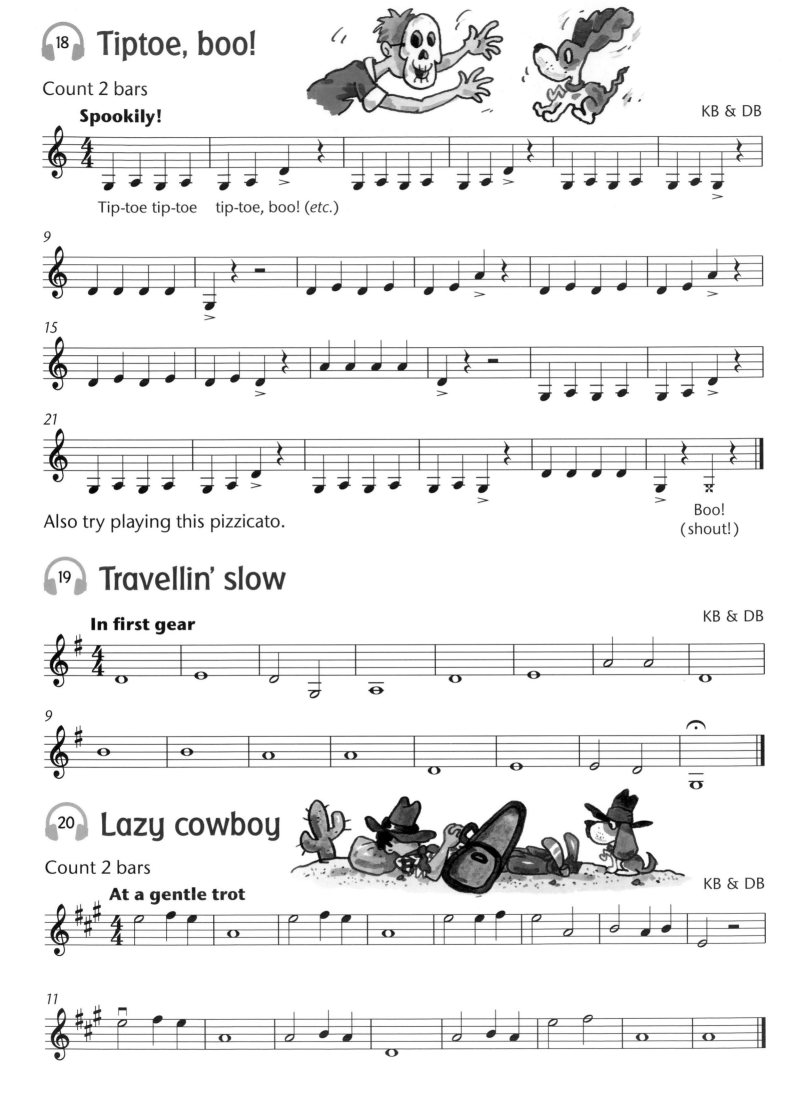

18 Tiptoe, boo!

Count 2 bars

Spookily!

KB & DB

Tip-toe tip-toe   tip-toe, boo! (*etc.*)

Also try playing this pizzicato.

Boo!
(shout!)

19 Travellin' slow

KB & DB

In first gear

20 Lazy cowboy

Count 2 bars

At a gentle trot

KB & DB

2nd finger

quavers
(eighth-notes)

21 Off to Paris

French folk tune

22 **Clare's song**

Count 4 bars

Gently

KB & DB

23 **City lights**

Gutsy

KB & DB

16

24 **The three friends**

Finnish folk tune

25 **Peace garden**

Not too fast

KB & DB

26 Summer sun

Count 4 bars

Gently

KB & DB

From now on, you'll be able to play both parts of the duets.

27 Phoebe in her petticoat

American folk tune

Swap parts when you do the repeat.

28 Ready, steady, go now!

KB & DB

50 Practice tempo

29 Cooking in the kitchen

KB & DB

Happy go lucky (for Iain)

Count 4 bars

KB & DB

31 The mocking bird

Gently like a lullaby

American folk tune

Now you can play the harder part of 'Someone plucks, someone bows' on page 5.

3rd and 4th fingers

Swap parts when you do the repeat.

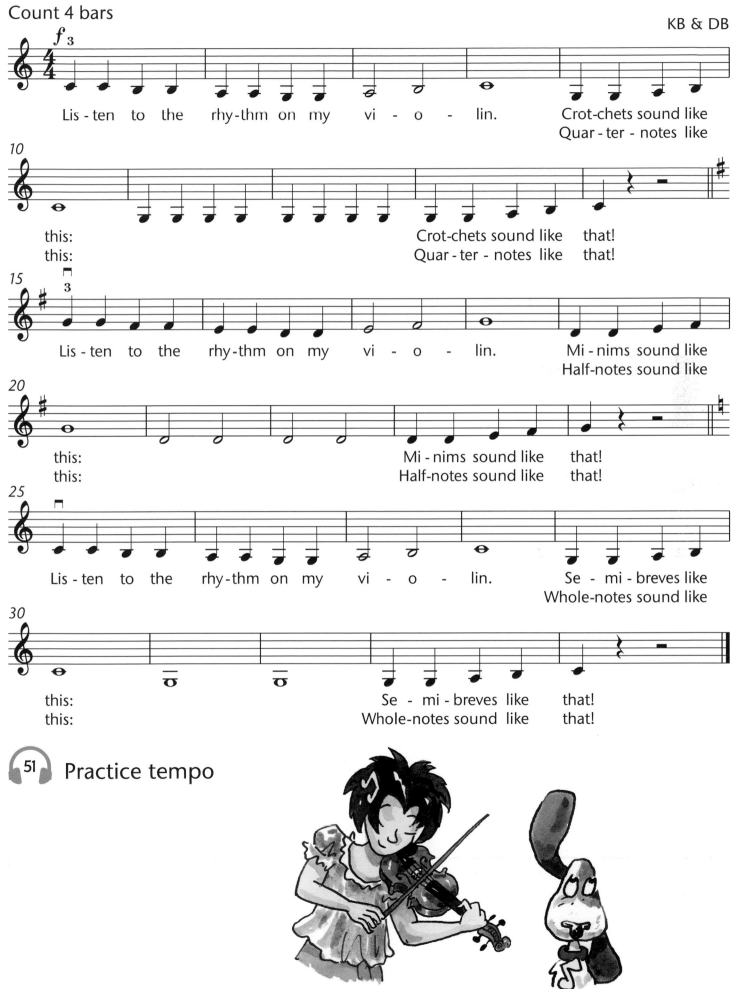

33 🎧 Listen to the rhythm

Count 4 bars

KB & DB

Lis - ten to the rhy - thm on my vi - o - lin. Crot-chets sound like
Quar - ter - notes like

this: Crot-chets sound like that!
this: Quar - ter - notes like that!

Lis - ten to the rhy-thm on my vi - o - lin. Mi - nims sound like
Half-notes sound like

this: Mi - nims sound like that!
this: Half-notes sound like that!

Lis - ten to the rhy-thm on my vi - o - lin. Se - mi - breves like
Whole-notes sound like

this: Se - mi - breves like that!
this: Whole-notes sound like that!

51 🎧 Practice tempo

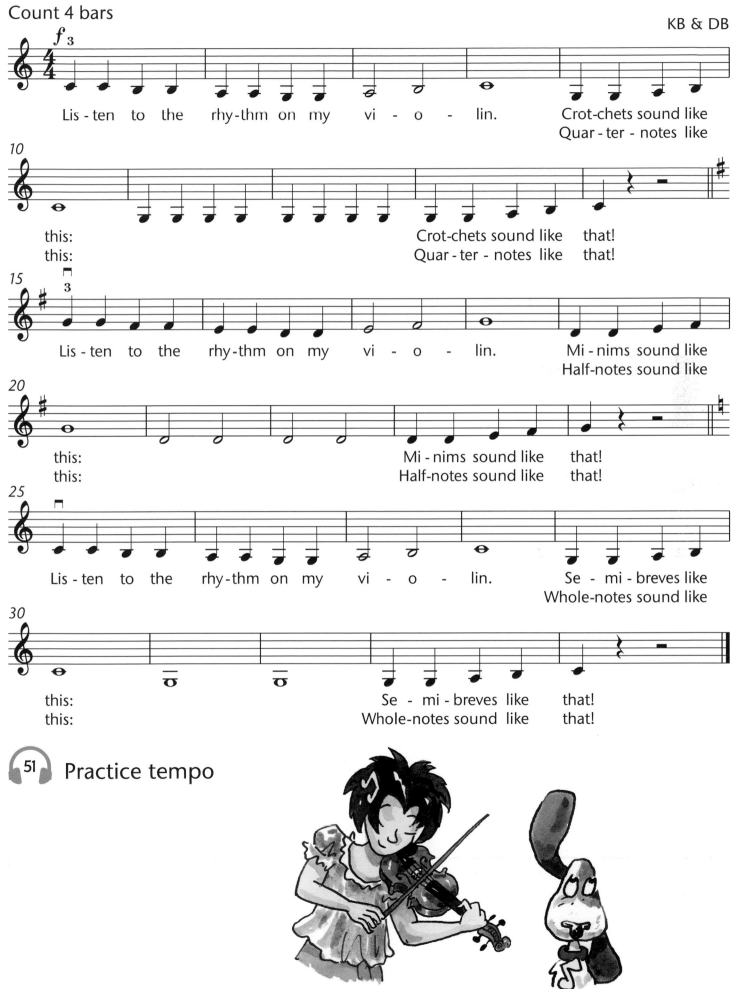

23

34 # Cattle ranch blues

Count 2 bars

KB & DB

Stompy

mf

7

cresc.

11

rit.

f

35 # In the groove

Count 2 bars

KB & DB

Swing

mf cresc.

7

f

11

mf cresc.

15

f

20

rit.

mp

Now go back to page 15 and play the harder part of 'Off to Paris'.

36 Stamping dance

Heavily

Czech folk tune

Try the harder part of
'Bow down, O Belinda' on page 4.

37 Distant bells

Count 2 bars

KB & DB

Slowly

mp

mf

rit.

p

Now go back to page 16 and play 'Clare's song', slurring three crotchets
(quarter-notes) to a bow.

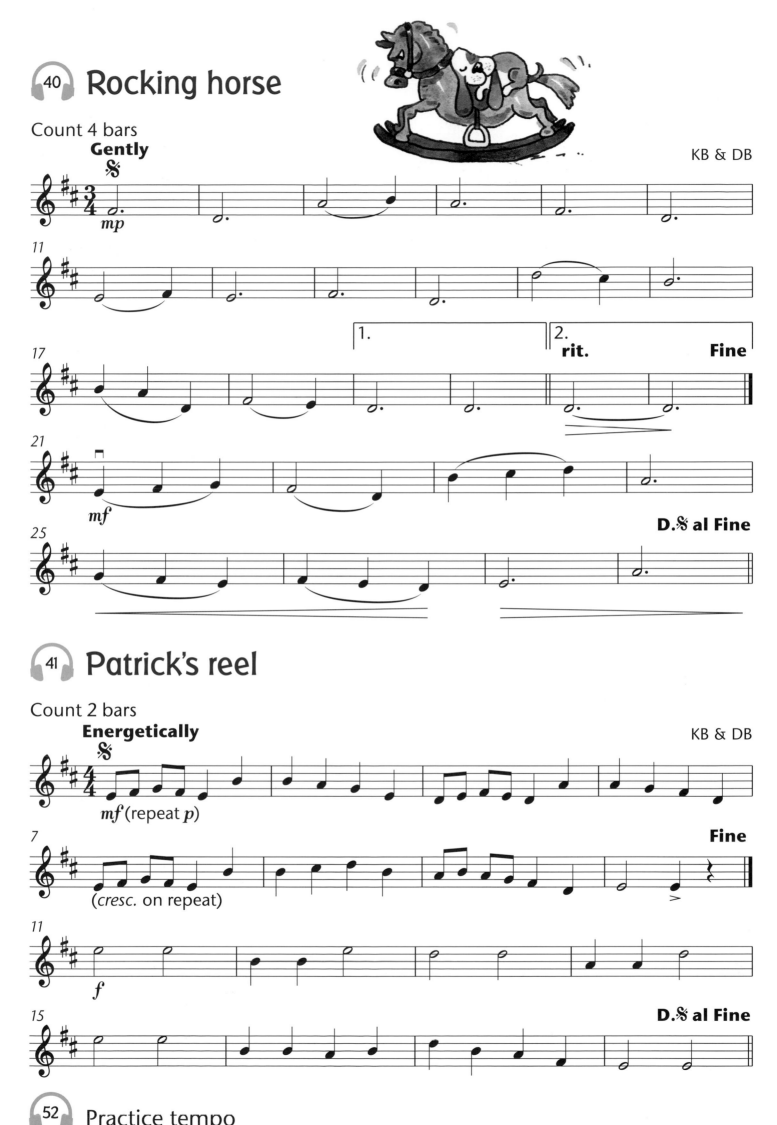

40 Rocking horse

Count 4 bars

Gently

KB & DB

11

1.   2.   rit.   Fine

17

21

mf

D.% al Fine

25

41 Patrick's reel

Count 2 bars

Energetically

KB & DB

mf (repeat p)

7   Fine

(cresc. on repeat)

11

f

15   D.% al Fine

52 Practice tempo

🎧 42 Calypso time

Count 6 bars

Carnival tempo

KB & DB

mf

11

15

cresc. *f*

20

1. 2. pizz.

mp

Now go back to page 13 and play
the harder part of 'Ally bally'.

🎧 43 Knock, knock!

Jokingly!

KB & DB

f

'Knock, knock.' 'Who's there?' 'Cook.' 'Cook who?' 'That's the first cuc-koo I've

4

heard this year!' 'Knock, knock.' 'Who's there?' 'Jes - ter.' 'Jes - ter who?'

7

'Jes-ter min-ute, I'll un - lock the door!' *ff*

Make up some other 'Knock, knock' jokes and play them on your violin.

Rocky mountain

American folk tune

Now try the harder part of 'Copy cat' on page 10.

🎧 45 Carrion crow

American folk tune

Try the harder part of 'Two in a boat' and 'London Bridge' on page 6.

🎧 46 Flying high

KB & DB

Count 2 bars

Try the harder part of 'The three friends' on page 17.

47 **Fiddle Time**

Count 4 bars

Easy going
$\%$ **(a tempo)**

KB & DB

53 Practice tempo

Music Fact-Finder Page

Here are some of the words and signs you will find in some of your pieces!

How to play it

pizzicato or pizz. = pluck

arco = with the bow

⊓ = down bow

V = up bow

> = accent

🎵 = tremolo

Don't get lost!

‖: :‖ = repeat marks

1. 2. = first and second time bars

D.C. al Fine = repeat from the beginning and stop at **Fine**

D.%. al Fine = repeat from the sign % and stop at **Fine**

rit. = gradually getting slower

a tempo = back to the first speed

⌢ = pause

Volume control

p (*piano*) = quiet

mp (*mezzo-piano*) = moderately quiet

mf (*mezzo-forte*) = moderately loud

f (*forte*) = loud

ff (*fortissimo*) = very loud

————— or *crescendo* (*cresc.*) = getting gradually louder

————— or *diminuendo* (*dim.*) = getting gradually quieter

Audio credits

Violins: Ros Stephen, Catrin Win Morgan, Marianne Haynes; *Viola*: Felix Tanner; *Cello*: Laura Anstee;
Piano: David Blackwell, Julian Rowlands; *Drums and percussion*: Andrew Tween; *Accordion*: Pete Rosser;
Guitars: Kevin Byrne, Dan Thomas; *Trumpet*: David Geoghegan; *Clarinet*: Nicola Baigent; *Flute*: Marta
Goncalves; *Voice*: Lin Marsh. *Engineers*: Ken Blair, Michael Taylor, Jeff Spencer, Ros Stephen; *Programmer*:
Edmund Jolliffe